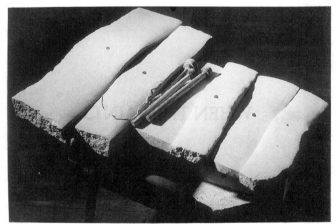

Sculpture by Brad Graves

JOHN TAGGART

WHEN
THE
SAINTS

TALISMAN HOUSE, PUBLISHERS
JERSEY CITY, NEW JERSEY

ISBN: 1-58498-002-8 (paper)
ISBN: 1-58498-003-6 (cloth)

Published in the United States of America by
Talisman House, Publishers
P.O. Box 3157
Jersey City, New Jersey 07303-3157

Manufactured in the United Sates of America
Printed on acid-free paper

Parts of this poem
have previously appeared, respectively,
in the following publications:
Chicago Review,
Xcp: Cross Cultural Poetics,
and *Hambone.*

Cover photograph used
by kind permission of Verna Gillis

FOR
BRADFORD GRAVES
1939-1998

Part One

The subject was roses the problem is memory
that was the subject roses piled to burn
intensity of a fire in summer intensity in intensity
ashes in a ring
pale rose hue of the rose ashes
that was the subject
the problem is memory the problem a problema
the problem a problema a problem to find
a problem to find the unknown
roses are known the cultivation of roses is known
to be flushed and full
like lips that have been carefully bruised
like lips that have been carefully brought to convulsion
and the danger of roses is known
Rilke died from a rose wound
the danger of roses a danger of cultivation
flushed and full
until a room becomes filled
until all the rooms of memory become one rose room
full of flushed lips and of their shadow.

A wish

more than
more than a wish desire
as strong as desire
as need
need's stronger
stronger than wish stronger than desire
need what's needed

for something to happen
in an enclosed place enclosed space

in a room.

Do the do
ain't seen nothing
till you see her do the do

nothing seen until she's been seen

curled up

something

something
she could do.

Thank you

not
nothing something

and for what comes after

word is found in what comes after
next word
necessary word
the word that I need.

There is no peace

no peace for the cultivator of roses

there is no peace

no peace for the cultivator of a single rose
only one of the more than one
single rose
secret rose
kept secret kept mystical
closed lips closed lips kept closed
there is no peace.

No other

piled to burn
all the more than one and the one

pale hue of the ashes
no other way
burning

that there may be
may be remembering of something else.

Ashes
ashes on the ground
ashes ashes all around

pale beauty
the beautiful burned to a pale beauty

pale rose and pale grey-blue

Rilke-like
these lines are like Rilke lines
some of these lines
those lines of a carefully cultivated beauty.

More than

more than roses

redbud

redbud and cherry
and one wild apple tree
the first to bloom these are the first

redbud and cherry and apple

a walk in the woods
is still a walk in ashes.

How to solve it

problem problema a problem to find

the word to be found between the lines
in the space between the lines

space of provocation

the space varies
the provocation also varies.

How to solve it

the word to be found between the lines

between combinations
lines are words put in combinations
combined to be remembered
to be memorable

lines are words put in combinations
a poem is a combination of lines
to write a poem is to make a discovery

combinations must be broken.

How to solve it
combinations must be broken
combinations of beauty
those beautiful and memorable combinations

broken or burned

space of provocation

in which the word discloses itself

next word
necessary word
the word that I need.

Rooms are the condition of the known
of what's known
condition of what I know

what I know
what happened to me
what happened happened in a room

in one room the one room of the chapel
what I know
to find the unknown
find the one room of the chapel

make the roof to fall in.

There are roses in autumn
in the cooler light of autumn
cooler and darker

a scattering of roses still in bloom
scattered continuation

continuation and concentration

concentrated
in the cooler and darker light of autumn.

Redouté

who kept his eye on roses

who kept the subject on the subject of roses

Redouté

the great painter of *Les Roses*

of the Provence roses

rosa centifolia

which must be lifted to be admired

one hundred

one hundred petals

enclosed by larger outer petals

one hundred pink petals

closely curled

Redouté

who kept his eye on roses.

No matter what

what

was

burned

what
stay burned.

There are roses in autumn
in the cooler and darker light of autumn

fullness of bloom
or beginning intimation

each with its grace each with its mercy

in that light

let them be piled to burn.

What is important
what is unknown is what is important
what is important to know

the cultivation of roses is known

to know = to see

to see what is in the room
what is important

to see what is in the room
what is after.

Part Two

The subject was roses the problem is memory
"all that is musical in us is memory"
memory is musical memory is musical in suggestion
suggestion of a progression
of a progression to a destination
the destination of music is harmony
everything joined to fit to fit together
closely fitted close harmony
which closes on a close which closes in on itself
there are other harmonies
there are harmonies which do not close
which close to open which close in open harmonies
which close with a question
with more than one
more than one a series of questions
the question of a progression without roses
to a destination without roses
the question of making a progression through ashes
to an unknown destination
the question of can I make up my mind.

Fear and fears the fear of memory

of being a slave to memory

calamity

this life = calamities
calamity after calamity of memory

the fear of no memory
runaway slave

who runs away from what to what.

Fear and fears the fear of memory

a slave to the memory of roses

calamity of a rose in bloom
in full and open convulsion
curled

calamity of burning
calamity
and fear of nothing thereafter.

A word can be a name
roses have names
rose of Provence the *centifolia* rose

one hundred pink petals
word and name for the petals

word and name for beauty

if one rose is burned
one word
word and name for beauty
will there be another
another word.

Sainte Colombe added a string

seventh string

Sainte Colombe added a string to the viol

six

six + one

added a vibration

six vibrations

six vibrations + one vibration

added a vibration and changed the vibration

added harmony and changed harmony

changed the destination of the music

the destination changed

became inward

secret

inward and secret destination.

Path and paths the path of memory

in a rose garden all paths lead to roses
to a destination of roses
to beauty

the roses must be burned down to the root
to and including the root

the root is desire
desire to eat
to eat beauty.

No way
and therefore wanted no eyes

want as need
need as need

question of need

the question is what do I need
what do I need I need to make up my mind.

Each with its grace
pale outer petals perfect paleness

imbricated
perfection upon perfection

each with its mercy
pale inner petals perfection of pale red
pale red inclining to purple

pierced by perfection
touched.

Sainte Colombe added a string
and changed the destination of the music
change by way of addition

six + one

one way
there are others
there can be change by way of subtraction
change by way of take away

take away

change.

In a rose garden all paths lead to roses
lead to and turn
return to that destination

in a burned garden there are no paths
there are only ashes
ashes everywhere

and no return to that destination

all paths lead to roses in a rose garden
lead to and turn

no return.

How can you say thank you

how can you say thank you to the roses
there are roses in autumn

how can you say thank you

to beauty that has been burned

Thank you how to say thank you

to a saint who wanted to be a saint

and who was

who was not Sainte Colombe

who wanted to awaken men from nightmare

who was not Rilke

rose perfume = the perfume of a saint's body

Rilke

the perfume poet par excellence

how to say

to a saint

who wanted to awaken men

who wanted to raise men from nightmare

saint of love

of a love supreme.

Saint

who takes delight in memory
who rises in the morning in pursuit of memory

overtaken

who is overtaken by tears

How to say thank you
to a saint

who wrote a poem
love poem a love supreme poem

some of the words of which
I've taken and changed

to find a word take away a word

what I have done
what I have done and what I am doing.

Overtaken by tears
you see nothing when you're overtaken
you're a saint

you're on the path of memory

going down the path and you're overtaken

you see nothing when you're overtaken

I do not want to be a saint
and I am not a saint.

Sainte Colombe added a string
changed the destination

there can be change by way of subtraction

it is no secret what I am doing

conference
from conference of birds to one bird

what one bird is doing

it is no secret

what I am doing.

In the middle of an island in the middle
led on by music

in the middle of my life

taken away changed

when the saints go marching
won't be in that number

one bird

one is an odd number
an odd bird then
odd bird odd enough song.

Part Three

The subject was roses the problem is memory
the problem is the train of memory
chasing the train
chasing the train of memory to its destination
its destination the chapel
all those stations in the chapel station
all those rooms
rooms are the condition of the known
all those rooms to one room
to the one child in the one room
child of pain
every progression suggests a problem
a problem of destination
a known destination
the chapel a known destination
child of pain a known destination
problem and question and more than one question
the question of an unknown destination
completely unknown
the question of making the roof to fall in.

Susceptible

for whatever comes in the ear
what comes in the ear

music

remembered
music

chapel music
screaming
screaming in the chapel.

Unforgettable that's what
what is

what is what is unforgettable

what is

what is unforgettable what is memory

all that is musical

what is in the chapel
what is in me.

"Je voudrais que mon amour meure"

stronger than want
than a wish
desire
strong as desire
need
stronger
need what is

what is what is needed

roof to fall in
child to die.

I'll be seeing you
you know where I'll be seeing you
you know all those places

you know = you see

you see all those old familiar places
and you see you

you = me

all those old places = one place

I'll be looking at the moon
I'm not looking at the moon.

Acknowledgment and acknowledgments
a page for acknowledgments
for acknowledgment of what has been taken
taken and changed

what has been quoted
poetry is the art of quotation
phrases comments cadences
in some instances without quotation marks

acknowledgment
poetry is the art of quotation
the art of cutting
cutting into
cutting into and around.

A page for acknowledgments
acknowledgment of error

error and errors

error of knowing
of being too knowing

error of not knowing
error of not knowing
what love is.

Too many all too many seeds in the air
like milkweed seeds
"beloved of imaginative children"

all too many milky seed words

ergo cutting
cutting into
around

ergo cutting

which clears the air.

What can be cut
roses can be can be cut and burned

you can be cut while cutting roses
Rilke was cut cutting roses

when roses have been burned
what's left what remains to be cut

what's left
yourself

you can cut yourself.

Before they were the Orioles
they were the Vibranaires
Sonny Til and the Orioles
first true rhythm and blues vocal group
first true rhythm and blues harmony
which opens
which closes on a close
true blue harmony
the Orioles opened the door
the Orioles closed the door
their biggest hit "Crying in the Chapel"
they cried in the chapel
you saw them crying
tears of joy
their tears were tears of joy.

Not so big a hit
"Back in the Chapel Again"

needed to go back and pray
went down
went down on their knees and prayed

burdens would be lighter
they'd surely find a way

again and again
back in the chapel in the need of prayer
back in the need of jokes.

Knock knock joke

Silvanus the teacher
knock upon yourself as upon a door

Silvanus the teacher
open the door that you may know what is

Silvanus the teacher
whatever you will open you will open

doorway without a door
which is the doorway of the chapel
doorway without a door.

Rhythm and blues harmony
minimal
minimal harmonic progression

from crying
from crying to praying in the chapel

in the chapel
back in the chapel again

minimal

going nowhere.

A musical joke a jazz joke
and a bird joke
a Charlie Parker joke
also a kind of knock knock joke

after a concert
Charlie Parker was asked
how much he cared about the critics
the critics who know so much

about as much as birds
he said as birds care about ornithologists

about as much.

Silvanus the teacher
walk upon yourself as upon a straight road

Silvanus the teacher
if you walk if you walk upon the road
it's impossible to go astray

if you = me

I walk the line between
lines

stray between

quite quite astray.

The point of a joke is a point

is pointed

something that could cut into and around

into and around memory

you need memory to remember the point

first a joke then the point

which is funny

needing memory to cut memory is funny

you could say the joke's on you

on you and in you

if you could remember

if you could you could cut it

you could be a cut-up

who cuts up who cuts into and around

who cuts it out.

You could say the joke's on me

me = me

on me and in me

chasing the train is funny
chasing the train to its destination
memory train
to its destination

to the chapel to the child of pain

chapel and child
chapel and child in me.

Part Four

The subject was roses the problem is memory
in the end the problem is a song
the problem a problema a problem to find
to find as in to extract from
extraction of a new song from what is in memory
a new song not an old song and not to the old harp
"Crying in the Chapel" is an old song
"Back in the Chapel Again" is an old song
not an old song
and not to the old harp
the old harp with eight strings
eight is too many
Sainte Colombe's seven is too many
too many strings and too many old time vibrations
too many vibrations twanging in the ear
a new song from what is in memory
what is extracted
extracted and mobilized
what is mobilized in the end
a new song the mobilization of a new song.

In the middle of an island in the middle
led on by music
charged to obey

in the middle of my life

obedience is to necessity

to what is needed

the roof to be made to fall in
child to die.

How to solve it

the solution is jokes
jokes and a joke from what is in memory

"God Bless The Child" is a joke
another musical joke and another jazz joke
a Billie Holiday joke

who's not his own
who's got his own

who's been blessed with his own pain

whose death would = a blessing.

How to solve it

"Better Git It In Your Soul" is a joke
Charles Mingus joke

get it out
better to get it down and so out

point of a joke is to bring about laughter
to bring the house down

your soul
is known by its dissatisfactions.

How to solve it

when we become conscious that choice
that choice must be made
choice's already made

saint's joke
St. Simone's foolish virgins joke

roof already fallen in
child already dead
chapel and child already out.

A love supreme saint
the saint said he had seen the father

mother of a love supreme saint
the mother said that meant he was going to die

to know = to see
to see the father = to die

death is no joke
in death there is no remembrance

or in death

there is only remembrance.

Simonides of Keos

who remembered the dead

who remembered where they were sitting

before the roof fell in

which was before they were dead

who put faces with places

who remembered the dead who they were

before they were dead

who saw them

who saw them again

saw them again in the rooms of memory

which is the art of memory

Simonides of Keos

who saw

who saw again.

Grateful
for a gravestone poet who saw
who saw again

a pleasant thought
that the not-dead dead may be grateful

Rilke wrote his own inscription
which was before he died from a rose wound

who wrote his own name
and the name of what wounded him
Rilke
and lust.

Inscription the art of inscription

grid on the stone
rectangles
each letter of each word on the grid
within each rectangle

the art of inscription = the art of poetry

the art is cutting
cutting what has been already cut

cutting into and around
the art is recutting the cut.

There are three

rough cut from the language quarry
rough cut slab of words

cut of the language of others
some of their words
quotation

the third cutting the already cut
cutting the recut

cutting
the quotation
free from the quotation.

There are two

obedience to the grid
each letter of each word on the grid

disobedience
each letter of each word
cut
cut free

free and abandoned dance of song

dance of an air
on air.

Death is no joke my friend died
a sculptor
a carver in stone
of a stone xylophone
stone xylophone carved in limestone
death is no joke my friend died
with wooden mallets
tied by a string
tied
to the stone
death is no joke my friend died
stone
not without tone
when struck deep tone and deep tones
marvelously distinct and deep tones.

With wooden mallets
tied by a string

let the string circle or loop
of string

let the string be broken

stone

let the stone be struck
let there be a transmitting of the tone
of distinct and of deep tones.

Head in hands in tears

in tears
you see nothing

you don't know what love is

a circle even
a circle in the sky
broken

even a circle in the serene sky

even
serenity.

Not an old song

elated
in its way
bye-bye to bye and bye

elegant
in its way
the recut cut
from what is in memory

exalted
if to be exalted is to have room

to have room to breathe.

And not to the old harp

three + two
odd and not
inharmonious number

which is not a number of strings
with broken strings or with no strings

not without tone
"the stone melodious"
to its deep tone to its deep tones
its distinct and deep tones.

A new song

thank you saying
thank you to the roses more than one

child who won't hear me saying thank you
to the child

to the saint to the other saints
taken and changed
as tears

thank you this is a new song
saying thank you.